Copyright © Nironence Moyo 2019

All rights reserved

All rights reserved. No part of this publication may be reproduced, or transmitted in any form, or by any means, without prior written permission from the author.

ISBN 978-0-620-85923-3

Edited by: Majority Ncube
Back Cover by: Z.Mhlaba Mkhulu
Front Cover by: Don de Dieu Bahaya
Proto Credit: Eye of Beauty
Mobile: +27 78 028 3818
WhatsApp: +27 78 028 3818
Email: neronence2@gmail.com
Facebook Page: Nironence Moyo Talks
Instagram: @nironence
Twitter: @neronence1
Website: www.nironence.co.za
Published in RSA

ACKNOWLEDGEMENTS

This book is dedicated to my two boys, Vincent and Emmanuel for the motivation they gave me. If it were not for you boys, I would not have seen the need to hustle the way I do. I might have easily given up the fight when the going got tough. You are the reason why I wake up with renewed energy everyday as I work on securing the best future for you. I remember vividly when I was heavily pregnant with Emmanuel; I used to go around doing presentations and at one time, I was so tired that I had to ask for a few minutes nap at one of my prospects' house before I could start the meeting. I had to leave you with a nanny at an early age and most people felt that I chose money over you. My aim was to make sure you get everything that you need without a struggle. I love you so much my boys.

To my late mum, you will always be missed.

To Nozi my young sister, thank you for teaching me to be a mother at an early age when I started taking care of you. I learnt so much endurance from that experience.

I would like to give thanks to my mentor who is also the editor of this book for all the advice, encouragement and support throughout this project. I appreciate your patience with the long late night calls as we pushed to make sure that this dream comes true. Your selflessness has contributed so much in developing me as a brand. I will forever be grateful.

To my pillars who have been working closely with me since the beginning, I love you so much and I salute you one by one.

Many thanks to must achievers for giving me strength whenever I felt like quitting. Together we are such an unbreakable force. It is never an easy task leading thousands of people but you made it achievable by being coachable and I am so happy to see you all achieving in numbers.

I would also like to thank Green World as a whole including the management at the Johannesburg head office; the training department; the finance department; the sales staff and the receptionists. Thank you so much for believing in me and helping in awakening the giant in me. I had never imagined myself being regarded as a brand and this company made it possible by providing me with the platform and all the required tools without demanding qualifications of any kind. On that note, I would like to thank my sister Virginia Moyo for introducing me to this life changing company.

To all the readers, thank you so much for purchasing this book. I hope it assists you to navigate easily towards your dreams. I love you so much.

Foreword

When Miss Nironence Moyo came to my office and asked me to write a foreword for her new book, I was amazed. This is a great honor for me.

I recall my memory for the past four years about Ms. Nironence Moyo, a lady full of business ideas, enthusiasm and passion. Throughout 4 years' endeavor, now she is a fast rising star of Green World, successful shop owner, powerful top leader and excellent motivator by reaching Three Star Manager level and becoming a millionaire. She created a historical record in Green World South Africa. As the management, we witnessed her legend of self-development. She does not only reach success by herself, I know the Must Achieve Team is with her. Many winners are from her team, and the team is united, committed and harmonious. Without her leadership, nothing like this would have happened. Niro is a determined person; she does not easily follow the ruts of others. While a lot of people are crying and complaining, she would prefer to solve the problem with some creative ideas. I think she knows that leaders are self-cultivated by facing many challenges and overcoming them with the team.

I believe her story will wake, inspire and uplift many people. Nowadays, we still have many people who do not know how to reach the financial freedom stage by Multi-level marketing. They struggle in the darkness, not seeing there is a lighthouse in Green World shining and guiding. Especially for some Green World distributors who don't know how to build the team and dream. This is a fair ticket to board on the plane of success. Pay your 100% attention to reading this book, you will find the answer. It is a book for those who are striving for the best in themselves and in others. It has the capacity to change lives because it shows us a way to develop who we are. I also strongly suggest to all the people who want to be successful leaders to read this book carefully. It should also become a popular and indispensable book for the business executives.

Finally yet importantly, I wish Niro and her team to reach higher targets and gain more income. May all the readers have a fruitful experience and get a better self. God bless us, God bless Green World.

Glory Guo

General Manager Green World

Introduction

The Journey to Self-discovery is an inspiring piece of work that carries invaluable life lessons written in simple English to accommodate every reader. It cuts across all groups and different aspects of life in a style that keeps you going until the last page. The author pours out her heart as she narrates her life story and shares her magic in turning predicaments around; moulding the perfect life she has always dreamt about. As you go through, you are sure to pick a number of inspirational points that will assist in a big way on your own journey.

Majority Ncube

JOURNEY TO SELF DISCOVERY

TABLE OF CONTENTS

CHAPTER 1

TURNING CHALLENGES INTO STRENGTH

In the summer of 1990, a small village of Huwana, Plumtree saw the birth of a girl. Though she came at a time the savannas of the area were starting to blossom and the mopanes showing their fresh buds, her real welcome to the world was with hugs and kisses of poverty. Her family was the poorest of the poor and at an early age, she had to be raised by her struggling grandmother and uncle who both had no stable source of income. Her predicament was worsened when she lost her father at the age of 5 and then two years later at the age of seven her beloved grandmother also passed away and she had to be raised by her aunt who was also raising her own children. The early schooling days were characterized by the inscription of poverty all over her tattered clothes and bare feet, not to mention the pain of frequently having to endure a growling empty stomach.

One can safely say, it never rained but poured for this young girl as the uncle who was providing the little that kept her going, passed on when she was eleven. Her next phase of life was to be spent with her even more struggling widowed mother who already had it hard trying to meet the ever-piling demands of the other siblings. At the new school in Tsholotsho, it was basically the same old challenges of being among the most destitute kids and the pain of being laughed at and teased by other kids for one thing or the other. Even though she had a tough time at school, she still loved learning so much and pushed herself harder every day to improve her grades to the extent that at Ordinary Level her impressed headmistress took her for a holiday at her house in Bulawayo, which was the first time for her to be in an urban area. Fortunately enough, she became one of the students who were identified to get assistance from a non-governmental organization and the pressure of school fees was eased through out her Ordinary Level.

Once she was done writing her final exams, she wasted no time joining the tough job-hunting task. It was a very bad time for trying to find employment in Zimbabwe as the whole country was experiencing an economic turmoil, with a lot of companies closing down and others relocating to countries with better economies. So it was a case of more people losing jobs at an alarming rate year in year out, making job hunting a tough call for someone fresh from school. She did not have many options left at her disposal but to join the hunt for greener pastures in neighboring countries and South Africa was the most viable one since most of her brothers and sisters had by then migrated there.

It was not going to be easy though settling in Pretoria, the capital city of Africa's largest economy. The expensive costs of accommodation did not make things easy for a young woman without any income in a foreign country. She was taken in by one of her brothers who offered her accommodation. The toil of trying to find a job without any previous work experience also weighed in on her efforts to establish herself. After many fruitless hunts for any kind of job, she was hired at one of the restaurants but without any experience she obviously had to start at the very bottom as a cleaner. It was a hard job but at least it got her set up with an income and before long many factors forced her to move out of her brother's place to find her own. She could only afford accommodation in a shack in the densely populated township of Mamelodi East. Her biggest worry all the time was safety since she had to always leave early in the morning to catch the train and only return late at night.

Still she did her job with so much dedication and it was not long before she was promoted from the cleaning section to do dessert preparation. She handled that new section with diligence that led to her next promotion to the chef's side to do grills. The new duties and challenges increased her confidence on the job and made her presence felt in the entire restaurant. Her capabilities, quick learning, and fast adaptation were noticeable from a distance and this caught the eye of the manager who gave her a chance to train as a server. A few weeks into the waitress training she was poached by a nearby newly established fish and chips franchise that needed a manager and before she knew it, her schedule had become a busy one as she was taken through her steps learning the ropes of the management post that basically involved running the entire shop. Even though the salary was a paltry R3000, it enabled her to move from the shack to rent a room in Mamelodi West.

It was during the time she was working at this restaurant that she fell in love with a man who later became the father of her children. Being new in love life she went into the relationship wholeheartedly and the excitement of being in a relationship swept her off her feet completely. She felt cared for and having a partner to share her problems and her life with. The relationship grew fast from level to level and it quickly got to a point where she fell pregnant with her first born son. It is then that things took a different turn.

The lovely boyfriend started developing into something else and sooner rather than later the sweet nothings they used to whisper to each other turned to angry shouts that shocked even neighbors. As the situation deteriorated and threatened to get out of hand, it was time to seek advice from friends and family. Many advisers encouraged her to hold on to the relationship citing that fights and other challenges were part of every relationship. They even went further to say it is normal for a man who loves you to beat you up sometimes if not always to express his love for you. It was their belief that as a wife you are like a kid to your husband, so the way that he treats his kids is the same way that he treats you. Having grown up without a father, she had a desire to see her child growing up enjoying the love of both parents. This forced her to try harder to make things work in a relationship that had turned sour before even reaching maturity. With time though the abuse turned physical which led her to be left nursing injuries from punches now and again and she had to call it quits on several occasions. Her biggest fear had caught up with her and she found herself at some point having to send the child home to her mother while she tried to settle in her new business after being fired from waitressing job. Her separation from the child was the most painful thing but she used it as a motivation to work harder so that she could be reunited with him again. This led to her ending up sharing a room with another girl, surviving by selling sachets of herbal tea.

Time is said to heal everything and often we are told that love is blind. These seemed to ring true for her as the bitterness and sad memories faded with time and she found herself back with her reformed lover. Promises of never repeating the past mistakes were made and soon the two lovers were pre-occupied with building their own heaven for three in their little haven. Their bundle of joy seemed to seal this dream perfectly after being brought back from Zimbabwe.

Things worked normal for a period long enough for the couple to be comfortable with having a second child and as soon as the second pregnancy was conceived the same old cycle of events played themselves all over again. This time around it really became uncontrollable and irreconcilable. A few years after the birth of the second child she even resorted to obtaining a protection order against the father of her kids fearing for the worst after a spate of very ugly altercations and many failed attempts at curbing the situation. The constant abuse also badly affected her new business of Network Marketing. Most of the time she felt dejected, lacking the necessary support from home and instead facing fierce enmity from the person who was supposed to be her pillar of strength. She undertook the painful decision of moving out of the home they shared; taking her kids along.

With all the burdens that a single mother of two faces she made a resolution that instead of crumbling under the weight of the burden, she will roll like a rock and crush all the obstacles on her way. Her determination to conquer grew, fueling her to double her efforts in the business all the time. She accepted that she was to be the father and mother of her kids and embraced the challenge with both hands. She realized that her happiness and that of her family was key to overcoming the daily chores of managing her team that was growing in numbers.

As a dedicated hard worker in Green World she moved quickly up the ranks building a huge productive distributorship while also growing her distribution centre into the biggest in Pretoria and surrounding areas. Her distribution Centre on numerous occasions produced the highest sales for the whole company in South Africa and the African region at large. It was not surprising when she reached the management ranks, which are the most cherished in the company. She became one of the top earners in a short space of time. She clinched the international star distributor of the year at the tenth year anniversary grand event in 2017. In 2018 besides reaching the honorary ranks and earning dividends from the company, she was given the ambassador role of Miss Green World. In 2019 on top of her role as the brand ambassador she was also appointed to be the face of the company in the advertising of the cosmetic range of products. She broke the record becoming

Green World's youngest millionaire at 29 years of age as of 2019.

She is now an inspirational figure among the youth and has received numerous invites to do motivational speaking around the country including at UNISA and sometimes sharing the stage with top motivational speakers like Linda Ntuli who used to be her role model. She has shown tremendous growth in motivation including organizing classy team events the last two of which brought the city of Pretoria to a standstill with car convoy parades before setting the classy Manhattan hotel alight with jubilation.

The name Nironence has undoubtedly become a household name among many at Green World, her team known as Must Achievers is proving to be one of the fastest growing brands. She has toured the world over with the company and featured prominently in events as either a speaker or trainer and an award recipient. She is simply one of the tried and tested leaders in recent years and it is a great pleasure to join her as she breaks down for us her formula of rising to the top and staying at the top.

CHAPTER 2

DON'T BE A PRISONER OF YOUR PAST

"I felt like a layer of mist that had blocked my vision for some time had been cleared and the relief that came with it became evident in every aspect of my life"

As we embark on this journey to self-discovery, it is important that we start at the beginning. My first step is to make you understand that there is so much weight carried by your past that if you do not handle it properly, it has the potential of holding you back forever. When we talk about our past every single person easily relates because we all have our different pasts that we can share.

Your past, whether good or bad must be simply understood as history and at some point in life must be left alone and the sooner that happens, the better. Some of us have marvelous pasts that we enjoy reminiscing about. It might be our early years in life, where we got all we wanted from our parents without a struggle. It might also be the previous employment or earlier relationships. The fact of the matter though is that no matter how good it was, it is not worth dwelling on forever. In fact if you look back at your past and discover that it was far much better than your present, it means you are not developing. That must give you all the reasons to work harder on making sure the future becomes a step or steps ahead. It must give you fuel, energy and consciousness to upgrade yourself.

There are others that have sad stories to share about their past like mine. In the previous chapter, I chose to take a brief reflection on my past through the eyes of a different person with the aim of sharing with you a proper emotionless narration. It was also very relieving to talk about my story without owning it. The mistake made by many people is to cling to the bad past using it as a curse upon themselves. The moment I realized that blaming all the things that have already happened in my life would never change my situation, I decided to walk away.

Walking away though is never as easy as a simple walk. You will first have to come to terms with whatever bad experiences that you encountered and accept that even though they cannot be deleted from your history, they are not needed in your future. Once you are convinced that the future provides you with an abundance of fresh pages where you get the chance to redefine yourself according to what you believe and see in you, then it will become much easier for you to leave your past in the past where it belongs.

Failure to do that means you will bear and carry around a tag that will constantly remind you of where you are coming from. During my schooling days whenever I was short of something like school fees, uniform or even small things like a pencil or a pen. I used to envy those kids who came from well off families and wished I also had both parents like them. Seeing my mother struggle to make ends meet became a motivation for me to study harder. I would find myself wondering why my father had passed on so early before he could do all these things for me. I would question myself why it had to be me who was in that situation while the other kids enjoyed the warm upbringing from their families. As I grew older though I got to a point where my focus shifted from the shameful upbringing and crying forever for my late father, to my studies. I realized that together with the rest of the kids, we were presented with an equal chance to study hard and get the desired results regardless of our backgrounds. There were no subjects that excluded those learners who were less privileged and therefore I had no reason to hang my head in shame. The moment that dawned on me, I got so much energy and determination to excel in my studies. I developed that burning will to perform to my best of abilities. I stopped viewing myself as one in a disadvantaged position and of course I was not. I was on the same platform as the rest as far as learning was concerned.

With this at the back of my mind I was able to convert my situation into an inspiration and thrived to prove a point about my capabilities. What I ate in the morning before going to school and the uniform that I wore did not matter anymore. I had awakened to the fact that I was at school for learning and my evaluation will always be results based not background based. Therefore, my advice to you is that, instead of viewing your past as a curse, you need to start viewing it as a teacher and an inspiration to change. My poor upbringing gave me many tough lessons and through those lessons I was inspired to go out there and curve out a better future for my kids. The experience of having a struggling single mother made me decide that I will be a better mother to my kids and best daughter to her. It gave me so much zeal and energy to aim high to avoid the same predicament for my children and my family as a whole.

Most successful people always have a sad past to share and in many instances when they do share their experiences their audiences feel like its motivational stories. The fact though is that some of these bad experiences provide a great learning curve to those who have the right level of alertness and mental readiness to pick the lessons. They are able to learn from the situations and detach themselves from their past moving ahead into the future with invigorated energy and spirit. Those who fail to do so will forever carry around this burden of the past and eventually they crack under the pressure and crumble. Their spirits are dampened by the anger about the past and their conscience is drowned by the blame they lay squarely on whatever did not go the direction they expected.

As a grown up woman, there were times that I felt valueless when badly treated in one way or the other. There were instances when I felt my background was the reason why I was not treated fairly be it at work or in my love life. On a bad day I would find myself wishing I had gone up to university and obtained a degree or some other higher qualifications. It was the bad past again trying to catch up with me and I never allowed myself to slip back. I taught myself to handle situations with maturity; I looked within and around myself for solutions. There are many adults however who are still stuck in their past up to this day. If you find yourself as an adult but still complaining about your parents, then you have a big problem. You are actually making your bad past hereditary because you are going to pass on the complaints, blames to your children, and guess who they are going to blame. All their complaints and displeasure will point straight back at you. It is therefore important not to leave it too long before starting your journey out of your bad past.

Many times I found myself moving out and back in with my boyfriend. The first time I moved out, I was extremely heartbroken after experiencing extreme emotional abuse and I thought I had made up my mind to take a different direction in my life. After a week or so I found myself listening to his apologies and before I knew it I was back in with him. The second, third, and fourth time I moved out after a series of physical abuse that left me nursing injuries. Every time I was beaten I had to lie to my friends and family about how I got the injuries. I had to make up stories that did not make any sense at all and I denied that I was being abused. Looking at my case, it is clear that I was stuck in the early days of our relationship when we still had love for each other. Even after many ugly confrontations I still believed that things would normalize and happiness would prevail again between us. I could not imagine life without this man. It just seemed impossible and all this was because I was stuck in the past. My focus was backward instead of forward and there was no way I could even imagine the future. Of course I was eager to have a stable relationship and a proper family but the way I fought for it was misread as desperation by my partner and that is how the abuse continued.

It was not easy to get to a point where I called it a day for good. When that finally happened, I felt as if a layer of mist that had blocked my vision for some time had been cleared and the relief that came with it became evident in every aspect of my life including business. It is only then that I was able to nature the belief within myself and my confidence grew. From this experience it is clear that a good past can also hold you back and make you fail to see opportunities or even seek them because your only focus becomes centered on restoring that past.

Another example of me holding on to the past was when I was fired from work due to ill health. Having worked as a waiter and later a manager, it became difficult for me to come to terms with the fact that I was jobless. The idea of finding another job and starting all over again did not sit well with me, I simply missed my previous job and hoped every day that I would receive a call informing me to return. I used to hire and fire people as a manager and I could not imagine myself going from shop to shop submitting my CV.

It was worse when I joined a Multi-level marketing company and had to go around selling herbal teas and other products. It looked like an embarrassing downgrade from my job as a manager. It took some serious training sessions, mindset adjustment and encouragement from the people in the industry for me to get to a point where I saw progress in what I was doing. Once that was achieved I started producing satisfying results. I started enjoying the freedom of working flexible hours, without a boss and benefiting from all my efforts. Beating deadlines that I set for myself was such a refreshing experience that left me with a glowing sense of being an achiever. Preparing for the next day's work made me feel in charge and because I was not taking instructions from anyone, this time I was my own boss. It was something I had not imagined possible the time I was still job-hunting.

Now we get to an understanding that our response to whatever situations we encounter in life especially those sad past experiences makes all the difference. The popular saying, 'if life throws lemons at you, use them to make lemonade', sums up this whole subject of the different situations we go through. It is a saying that teaches us to make do with whatever we have. It encourages us not to succumb to trying times and always be ready to deal with whatever situation we encounter. As they say, 'whatever doesn't kill you will make you stronger'.

I chose to add sugar to my lemons rather than weeping over them to turn to oranges and I encourage whoever is still holding on to some bitterness of yesterday or yesteryears to take the same advice. Let no situation stand on your way to success. If your past shaped and defined you, reshape and redefine yourself for a better future. Understand that you never chose your past but the future is in your hands.

CHAPTER 3

MIND-SET AND BELIEF SYSTEM

"It is always going to be a difficult task to embrace new things that are out of our belief and scope. It has to start with a willingness to learn and understanding that the reason we do not know certain things is simply because we have not learnt them or we haven't got exposure to them"

"Lack of flexibility in our thinking patterns on the other hand limits our brain and once it is limited we are limited."

Of utmost importance in dealing with situations and the ability to free yourself and move ahead is the issue of mindset and belief systems. Our thinking patterns and beliefs are programmed by our environment. The same way that we learn the language, culture and practices of the people in our environment, we also automatically fit in their belief system and thinking patterns. As we grow up though it is up to us to mature and explore other ways of thinking and beliefs.

What you think and believe in has so much contribution towards your behavior, practices and habits and ultimately in determining your course of action and direction. Growing up in Tsholotsho I was surrounded by people who had been hardened and toughened by poverty to an extent that they did not care anymore. Their daily battle was the battle for survival, whereby people worried day in day out about their next meal. In years of good harvests most will have surplus food and will use it to trade for livestock with villagers from other areas. That would be considered a great achievement in the area and so life revolved around those practices. Even though some people had great ideas for developing themselves and venturing into big businesses, they were incapacitated by lack of resources and the infrastructure of the area. Remember electricity was not available; no proper road network and no guaranteed water supply. Therefore, this meant any idea of a big business venture was inconceivable under such circumstances.

I grew up in this type of environment, and this is the kind of mind-set that I adopted. Most of the youth of the area would fall into this way of life immediately after going up to ordinary level. A large number dropped out of school at different stages for different reasons and mostly it was lack of funds for school fees. Due to scarce employment many had to cross borders to neighboring countries like Botswana and South Africa in efforts to survive. Others lost hope and just stayed in their parents' homes relying on the support of other siblings to keep going. Young girls resorted to early marriages where they became homemakers while their husbands who were most often much older than they were, went to find work outside the country. No wonder I also got married at an early age, it was a fashionable thing back at home.

Then there were those youngsters that you would not be able to point out their actual business, they would be seen roaming around in the local business center with absolutely no particular direction. They resorted to drinking, smoking, and often coming together in organized groups without a clear mandate. These always became the first suspects whenever there was a crime committed in the area, and in most cases they did not just become suspects but ended up behind bars. This same pattern of behavior has been in existence for so many years and continues today with many slight additions and subtractions of no significance.

So basically my thinking was programmed along those lines when I grew up, and it was not surprising when I found myself joining the many that had crossed the border to South Africa, it was the norm. When I had problems in my relationship the advice that I got was about being patient with my man. This was all we had learnt as we grew up, we were taught that patience is the backbone of every relationship and it strengthens marriages. However this did not seem to work in my case. I exercised so much patience and hope but it was all effort down the drain. It did not yield the desired results. This is not to say it doesn't work. It does work perfectly for some people; it just did not work for me. That is why I ended up breaking the norm and leaving the relationship. I had realized that I was trying so hard to do the right thing in the wrong place that it was not going to work even if I had dedicated my entire life to being patient with this man. So this was a lesson to me that not all you believe in will always work in your favour. There are times when the mind-set has to be adjusted and the belief system has to change according to the situations at hand.

Beliefs surrounding work life and business also had to be overhauled at some point. I grew up knowing that the only way to come out of the poverty situation was to get a job and work hard. During the time when I was working as a manager I felt I had made it in life. I was being paid R3000 a month, sharing a space at an apartment as my home in South Africa. I could not afford to own a car. After sending some money to my mother back home, I was left with very little to take me through the month. Still I saw nothing wrong with that. I believed I was doing the right thing, in fact the best as a manager. I was the envy of many of my home girls even though I had nothing to my name. Just by being a manager, I considered myself, as somebody who had a nice job and even back home it became known that I was working as a manager. Nobody ever worried about me making meaningful progress in life. Everybody was content with me being in that position.

When I was fired due to ill health, I was obviously devastated and so were those close to me. I felt that things had fallen apart and my life had come to a standstill. Once I had recovered from sickness, I was back on job hunting. I was hoping and wishing I would again get a job as a manager. I could not think of doing anything besides a job. As far as I understood things, there was no way I could venture into business since I did not have start- up capital. Business for me meant running a grocery or bottle store back in the rural areas, which were the businesses that I knew and understood with most of the people from my home area who were considered to have made it in life, running such businesses. Others had gone into the transport industry ferrying goods and people from their different bases in the Diaspora back to Zimbabwe. All these businesses for me required large amounts of money to get involved. It appeared as if business was something out of the question for me as I carried my CV around desperate to be hired as a manager.

When my sister offered me a business opportunity on the street in the form of Network Marketing, I did not make any serious considerations about it. I bought products that I needed from her and my main concern was to be healed from my sickness. It took so much persistent persuasion from her for me to finally attend the presentation. Even when I signed the joining form, I had not seen the business that they were talking about. It did not make any sense at all, so I just signed because it only cost

R120 and I liked the fact that I was going to buy the products on discounted prices as a member. Being in constant contact with the person who signed me, I attended more presentations, listened to testimonies and before long I found myself willing to give it a try. It still did not sound like a business though to me. To cut a long story short, I did this business successfully to a point that I ended up achieving things that I never imagined one day that I would ever achieve.

The point that I want to emphasize here is that your mind-set and beliefs ought to be flexible at other times in your life. Our brain normally thinks around our everyday life and that becomes our level of understanding in life. You can spend the rest of your life cut out from some of the best things because you never got exposure to them. Alternatively, when you got that exposure, you were not flexible enough to allow your brain to acclimatize itself with the new item or concept. I feel like taking a whip and whipping myself whenever I look back and realize that I had to be begged numerous times to take up a business opportunity that completely changed my life. I cannot stop asking myself what was wrong with my brain. So my main problem was that I had a poor understanding of what business was and at the same time was not ready to allow myself indulgence into new information. Surround yourself with positive minded people in your circle and always make sure its people who push you to be better. Believe in yourself more than anyone else.

The question that arises is; how many people out there have lost opportunities and chances to change their lives because of such rigid thinking ways. So many people still exercise this kind of thinking in different aspects of their lives. It is always going to be a difficult task to embrace new things that are out of our belief and scope. It has to start with a willingness to learn and understanding that the reason we do not know certain things is simply because we have not learnt them or we do not have exposure to them. When we have that understanding then we are open to exploration and adventure. Once we allow ourselves to learn new things all the time we get the opportunity to put our brain into full use and it is the brain that expands our world and multiplies our chances of success in any field. Lack of flexibility in our thinking patterns on the other hand limits our brain and once it is limited we are limited.

We know scientifically that our brain is in charge of executing and coordinating almost all the functions of our body. With that understanding we therefore have to agree that it has to stay competitive in the best way possible. That competitiveness can easily be derived from exposure to new challenges and embarking on diverse avenues in life. The same way that our mind-set and beliefs are programmed by our environment as we grow, can be adopted to reprogram and re-adjust as we encounter new things, meet new people and live in new environments.

Choose wisely the people that you hang around with. If you have big dreams and aspirations, it does not help to share them with people who are hopeless and negative because at the end of the day they will crush you and drag you down to their level. I have observed a number of times when some people attend top class motivational sessions. They come out of there motivated and in a conquering mood. When they get back to their friends and family, their bubble is immediately burst and all the excitement lost. If you are working and earning around R20 000, you must not be found spending too much time with people who aspire to earn that amount. It gives you a sense of being at the top and no challenge at all.

On the other hand if you spend time with people earning around R50 000, you immediately realize how much room for development you have. Eventually you will also find ways of upgrading to that level. I used to wish I could earn around R5 000 and it looked like a far- fetched dream at that time because most of the people around me were earning less than the R3 000 that I was getting. When I came to Green World, I found out that there were people earning around R60 000 in a month, and that was twelve times the amount that R5 000 I wished to earn. So the power of association can never be over emphasized. The influence that we get from people around us has the power to make or break us.

It is vital that you understand the people around you, so as to be able to differentiate between the advice that adds value to you and one that needs to be discarded. Big dreams do not mean anything to people who do not dream. They just seem like madness to them and if you give them enough time they will definitely convince you so. When you have taken the route to success and greater things in life; there are close people that you need to sacrifice and do away with. It frees you and helps you focus. In whatever project that you undertake, it is important that you adjust your mindset at the same time bringing yourself to a point where you have total belief in its fruition. It makes it easier for you to create a clear image of what you want through visualization.

CHAPTER 4

VISUALIZATION

"Visualization provides you with navigation tips and helps you avoid some of the obstacles that might be encountered along the journey"

"If your vision is to become a millionaire, your language automatically changes from 'if I become a millionaire' to 'when I become a millionaire'"

In this journey to self- discovery it is important for you to create a clear vision of where you are heading. Visualization gives you an idea about your journey and your destination. It provides you with navigation tips and helps you avoid some of the obstacles that might be encountered along the journey. When you have a clear vision of what you want to achieve, you are inspired to work towards it and you cannot afford to mistake it for something else because you know exactly what you want. At the back of your mind you will always have vivid images of what you want to achieve and that is what will give you fuel to keep on going even when to others it seems dark.

Financial

You therefore need to visualize yourself in all aspects of your life. For example, financially you need to be able to see yourself somewhere within a certain period. Let us say you make projections for the next five years or decade or whatever period. You need to picture yourself in that future period having achieved your desired financial status and living the life of your dreams. If your vision is to become a millionaire in the next five years and clearly outlined in your mind, your language automatically changes from 'if I become a millionaire' to 'when I become a millionaire'. This is because your vision has helped you to conceive your dream and there is no slightest doubt in your mind that you will achieve it. It is only a matter of time before it materializes. Having a vision though must be understood in a way that does not bring your life to a standstill. Some things that need to be done along the way have to be done.

My vision is to own a beach mansion but that did not stop me from buying a small house that I live in at the moment. It is because I understand my vision is long term and in between now and then life has to go on. I must have a place to live with my kids until that time. Therefore, every day when I wake up in this house, I know it is a stepping-stone towards my mansion, and the journey continues. Owning this house even draws my dream mansion closer as a confidence booster. The small things that you achieve along the way have significance in building the momentum in your journey.

Career

Career wise also it is important to create a vision as to where you want to take yourself in years to come. The vision will more than help you cement your stance towards your desired upgrade. Do you still remember as a child when your teacher used to ask what you want to be when you grow up? Students used to come up with different careers like teacher, doctor, nurse etc. For many it was just wishes as it quickly faded as soon as the class was over. There are those however who visualized their careers to an extent that they later went on to pursue them and lived their dreams happily. So we can take great lessons from those kids who ended up pursuing the careers they envisioned in their childhood days. The path that they followed from there was one that would eventually yield their desired results. It means they went on to improve their focus on particular subjects in accordance with their course of vision. The universities and colleges that they went on to attend were obviously ones that furthered their knowledge on their respective fields of interest. In similar fashion that is how we need to visualize our careers. My vision is to expand my business empire in the next ten years making sure I create numerous streams of income so that by age forty, I can be able to retire and focus on strengthening my spiritual life. Even though I lead a strong spiritual life, it is part of my vision to devote the later years of my life to more work around that area.

The fact that careers go hand in hand with income and of course financial status provides a reasonable amount of motivation in keeping your focus fixed on your vision and the results that come with achieving it. Your career vision can be linked together with the earlier segment of financial visualization as they complement each other in many ways. A great career can help you achieve great financial standing while in the same way; good financial standings make it easy for you to pursue your desired career.

Health

Later in your life your health status will definitely require extra attention. As the body ages, there are many processes that start to fail leading to a development of many different types of diseases. We have all encountered ailing adults nursing diseases that they never used to have. It is up to you when you visualize your health status to make sure your vision accommodates the best possible plan that will help you curb some of the most common diseases that come with age like arthritis, hypertension, visual problems, brain problems and many others. For health visualization though it is vital to have segments of your vision according to the progress in years since for many diseases, prevention is better than cure. Without good health all the other visions that you have about your future are likely to be impossible. There is no work and definitely no joy without health.

Personal Growth

As much as we are fighting this battle of alleviating poverty and scarcity mindset, the bigger goal is the attainment of the everlasting life as stated in John 17:3. My retirement will definitely not be about sitting on the couch and watching television throughout the day. There is obviously going to be more focus on my spiritual life and reaching out to more people and teaching them about the only true God and the one that he sent, so that they obtain the ultimate goal, which is everlasting life. I visualize myself as a very busy person after retiring and when that is achieved my achievements would be perfectly sealed.

Recreation

On my list of visions I also have recreation. I have the understanding that recreational activities including travel, entertainment, leisure and games play an important part in the general life of a human being including brain health and development not to mention giving the body time to relax or some form of exercise. That is why I visualize myself touring the world to all the destinations on my list. Traveling enlarges one's horizon and even gets you exposed to new knowledge, which in turn stimulates one's brain. I will set aside an annual budget for the whole family's touring expenses. My house will also definitely have a well- furnished study for reading and writing purposes. I will also see to it that I erect a tennis court, gym and a mini zoo within the yard. I also want to create a gallery where I would be able to store all my collections from around the world.

Giving back to the Community

As a person who grew up in poverty, I understand that many people who are considered destitute just need to be given hope to find themselves and get back on their feet. Ever since I started the Multi- level marketing business, I have visited a number of communities including the well off and underprivileged with the aim of inspiring them to always be eager to take up new challenges. Since I have acquired presentation, training and motivational skills, I aim to help equip all those who are willing to learn. I believe this is a more empowering thing than giving handouts. Once I restore hope to the hopeless, I also share with them the business that I am doing ensuring that they do not fall back again.

Relationships

I view healthy relationships as great treasure in my life. I still remember very well when I started doing business without any of my family members. I worked with total strangers who trusted and believed so much in me that I never felt out of place or stranded. These people gave me so much confidence and peace of mind. It has always been such a great feeling to wake up in the morning and start receiving and making calls to my team members exchanging ideas on how to tackle the day's work. Some of the biggest achievements that I have attained would not have been possible without the efforts and good relationships that I share with my team. Together we have organized and hosted some of the best events in the history of MLM. Some of the events took days of planning, some even months and all this time the team would be working together to make sure everything falls into place. It is for this reason why I have a vision of strengthening these relationships even more in future. I would like to see them in my celebrations, my trials and even in my funeral. I promise to also do the same for them as long as I live.

Besides good relationships with my business partners, I also have a vision of creating strong family bonds. I would like to see my family coming together regularly to spend quality time and share ideas. I do believe my success will be more meaningful if it is shared with the whole family. So one way or the other, my family would be constantly presented with this vision until they all grasp it. Of course most of them already have other ways of making money, but I just hope to help them add MLM as another stream of income. Remember I do tours to different places to offer free information on how to improve our lives. Therefore, I should not have a problem sharing such opportunities with my family including extended family. As a mother of two boys it is part of my vision to see my relationship with them grow and extend to their future wives and kids.

All these visions need to be followed up with a clear action plan including set goals in order for them to roar to life and be able to generate inexhaustible excitement throughout the journey. Besides that they get reduced to mere wishes like those kids who just express their career wishes to the teacher just because he has asked and get done and over with it as soon as possible. For the vision to materialize it needs a proper action plan that will give direction and make sure effort is applied accordingly.

CHAPTER 5

FOLLOW A CLEAR ACTION PLAN

"For every action there is a reaction, therefore take massive action to produce massive results"

Now that you have a clear enough vision, it is imperative that you lay down a clear course of action that will guide you throughout your journey. Your vision without action remains a wish and it will never implement itself. It is time to roll up your sleeves and get down to real work. Understand that you are now taking those glamorous images that you have created in your brain about your future and bringing them into fruition. The action plan therefore must be a watertight one to ensure that your vision is not demolished by whatever hazards that might be there. Your implementation at its early stages must be treated with the same care that is given to a newborn baby. It is important that you stand firm and protect your vision all the way. Do not let anyone steal your vision or crush it in any way. For example my vision of a house on the beach encountered some attacks as soon as I brought it to the attention of the world. Some of these attacks came as genuine questions from people around me while some were said behind my back. I also got advice from concerned people trying to convince me to reconsider my vision, because according to them, it was unachievable.

I treated all this in the same way, whether it was advice, genuine questions or useless talk behind, it was all aimed at stalling my vision. So I offered everyone bold confident answers that made them see that it was mission impossible to convince me otherwise on my vision. It is important to be bold about your vision all the time and never get to a point where you are unsure of how to handle critics. The following steps that I have outlined will go a long way in keeping you on the right track towards achieving your vision.

<u>Take bold steps</u>

As I have already stated, make sure you show a bold stance in whatever you do to an extent that you scare the daylights out of your potential vision crushers. The bold steps can be emphasized by your aggression and massive action as you take off with your project. It is important that as much as you are driven by the burning desire to reach your goal, you are actually the driving force behind its implementation. You need to unapologetically own it and make it become part of your day-to-day lifestyle. It is vital that you enlarge your vision to a size that scares even you the owner. Achieving starts by aiming high. If you aim low you are likely not to hit anything and even if you do hit you will obviously not be satisfied with a low target. So your boldness must be seen in aiming for the moon so that when you miss you fall on the stars.

Be creative

Your creativity will come in handy whenever problems are encountered along the way. It is of vital importance that you always come up with an alternative plan if plan A did not work. The idea is to make sure you keep moving forward no matter what happens. Therefore, your thoughts must not only be straight but also wide and far-reaching in terms of exhausting available options. Do not be limited by the plans and goals that you have already placed down. Be able to play around with them while still keeping on track for the bigger target. If you are creative enough you will never run out of ideas. You will also be able to convert some of the obstacles you encounter along the way into building blocks instead of stalling your progress. Your creative mind must be able to takeover where everything else stops. The strong will to go for your vision must also be constantly tapped to supplement your creativity. It is often said that, 'where there is a will, there is a way'. Your unwavering will must assist you to create ways and more alternative ways. Do things that have never been done before and do not be afraid to flop and learn. Just do more.

Take full Responsibility

As the owner of your vision, you need to take full responsibility because you are the only one who knows what you want. The vision exists in your mind not in anybody's mind so it would be disastrous to entrust someone with it. I have a clear vision of my beach house and that is why I could not take advice from people who had no idea of what they are talking about. While people are busy talking about the estimated expenses of the house, my responsibility is to focus on accumulating the actual money that I know I will need. Obviously I have already done all the necessary research that is why I am working on widening my streams of income to make sure I have no problem when the time comes. So taking responsibility means you have to create the conditions conducive for the fruition of your vision. It does not help in any way to have a vision and not pave the way for its fruition. You need also to be mindful of some pitfalls along your path. The following are some of the things that you should be wary of:

Be mindful of your thoughts

Whatever your brain conceives is going to determine the course of action that you are going to take. As much as your thoughts can inspire you to success, bad thoughts can destroy you and crush your dreams. It is important to always have positive thoughts all the time. Make sure your vision is not pushed out of your mind by negative thinking that will always creep into your mind. There will be times when you are tempted to believe the prophets of doom. Maybe on a particular day you are so broke that you cannot even buy yourself bread and when you look at your vision, it looks like insanity. You need to be able to treat being broke as a temporary current situation while your vision is a permanent future. Many people fail to pursue their dreams simply because they rule themselves out based on the present. Don't allow negative thoughts and small problems chase away your big vision. Whatever you believe, you become.

Be mindful of your words

Words have the ability to create and we need to guard against cursing ourselves with the words that come from our mouths. Many people believe they have been cursed in their lives but their real curse is what they say about themselves. People complain about being poor, being failures, being broke, being out of business and so on. They say these things repeatedly until they believe them automatically becoming crippled.

I remember when I was introduced to the business world I was taught to be always positive when talking about my business. If anyone asks how business is going, my simple answer is that it is booming. With this simple answer you can get yourself a new client because people like so much to be associated with things that are performing well. How would you expect to get a client after complaining about your business? It is the nature of people not to want any association with things that are failing. Therefore, every time when you complain about the business being down, complaining about how expensive it is to handle the day-to-day costs, you must know that you are actually driving your clients away and personally destroying your business to the ground. The point is never get to a stage where you end up cursing your vision with negative complaints. It is normal for things not to go as expected and at the same time, it is your responsibility to bring them back on track. Do not massacre your vision with your mouth. Remember while you are busy complaining about it, someone out there is tackling the same situation and succeeding. Instead of complaining and cursing try the opposite.

Action it

It is important to create some urgency in the process of implementation of your vision. Try by all means to avoid procrastination. When you delay implementation, the excitement around the idea starts to fade and chances are high that at the end of the day the idea ends up being shelved forever. It is your responsibility as the owner of your vision to make sure excitement stays in the same levels. This, you ensure by putting into action those ideas that will create the momentum and maintain it. Again do not be afraid to do those small things as they bring you closer to your main focus. When I bought my house, some people might have thought I had finally given up on the vision of a beach house. For me it was a way of putting my vision into action because planning without action is just like wishing. All the time I did not hesitate to tell them that this was just the beginning of great things. It was just a stepping-stone. For me the confidence that I got from that action is just unexplainable. The motivation will definitely stay with me for a long time as I move towards my vision. For a person coming from such a background as mine, that is such a huge achievement. I never imagined myself owning a property in an upmarket estate, so when I made that purchase it was confirmation that anything is possible. So as I go forward, nothing is going to deter me. Action is a great affirmation of your visions. It affirms them to you and to the people around you; hence clearing any doubts. So in whatever you do, never delay action. Make it a habit to do things and before you know it, you will be within reach of your vision. While small steps that you take everyday help you to get closer to your vision, bear in mind also that for every action there is a reaction. Take massive action in order to produce massive results.

CHAPTER 6

MLM TO MY RESCUE

"There is no one business model that receives so much scrutiny and backlash from both the labour force and the employers across the world than Network Marketing"

Multi-level marketing or network marketing is one of the oldest and very effective systems for the distribution of products, information and other services. However for so many years it has been misunderstood and continues to be interpreted with confusion and too many mixed emotions. There is no one-business model that receives so much scrutiny and backlash from both the labour force and the employers across the world than Network Marketing. Many professionals always choose to view it as a career for those who are not academically enhanced and hence the widespread belief that it is for those who are desperate. On the other hand when employers come across a Network Marketing company, they see a threat to their trusted and experienced labour force. At the end of the day there is a consensus that depicts the business as a bad unreliable business. This is the kind of rhetoric that I was fed by those close to me when I showed interest in the industry.

When I finally signed up with one of the companies though, it became an enlightening experience as most of the myths that I had come across got debunked with every passing day. In my initial stages with the company I got many warnings that I was going to be scammed and lose money. I failed to find relevance in this piece of advice since I did not have any money. So this was useless advice. After spending a few years in this industry, I have come to the conclusion that it is the best business for people with big dreams and zeal to contribute to a different world. The important thing is to pick a company that is genuine with good products and services plus an excellent compensation plan. Once you have that under check then you are good to go.

Once I got involved I chose to focus my efforts on working the company system and producing results. The products had healed me from my sickness of many years; I had developed confidence in that area. Therefore, the next step was to just run with the business.

While it is important to do a proper background check, it is also vital that you do not spend too much time on that area. The rest of the things you will get to know and understand with time. From my experience in the industry, I can tell you that it is highly impossible to understand most things about a MLM company in a short space of time especially the compensation plan. Most MLM companies have wide compensation plans that will take you months if you are to dissect every detail about them. Once you are involved it is easier to take a closer look and have a better assessment of everything about the company. I would therefore advise those aspiring to venture into this kind of business not to waste too much time and end up being researchers instead of networkers.

What you can rest assured about though is that most of the time as long as the company is genuine, it has already been tried, tested and trusted so you are not going to start over again to try it out. Once you are satisfied with the company history and compensation plan what is left is simply to work the system. Taking too long analyzing every detail of the business and not doing it will surely not give you any results but just regrets. Now let us look at some of the benefits of doing Multi- Level Marketing as compared to other types of businesses.

Affordable start-up and low risk

 Firstly the start-up fee for most MLM companies is affordable. This is an advantage for those people who want to start businesses but do not have capital. Many people give up on dreams of ever owning businesses because of high amounts of money needed for start-up. This makes MLM an ideal business for the millions of entrepreneurs who are eager to change their lives. There is no worry of losing money in case things do not go according to plan. The expenses that often confront up- coming businesses such as daily running costs and rentals are greatly reduced as most companies set up and manage their offices. As a new member, you get to settle in business quickly and start seeing progress.

For me MLM became an answered prayer as I was financially lacking to be able to have a reasonable business of my own. So when I was offered an opportunity to sign up with a multi-billion dollar company for only R120, there was nothing more that I could ask for. It was the best opportunity I was ever presented with in my life. It is the best business as it accommodates all including the disadvantaged.

Flexibility

Another good thing is that there are not too many terms and conditions set to determine who qualifies to do the business. Most MLM companies do not care about things like academic qualifications, nationality, race, retirement age, physical disability and things like that. This means individuals are given a fair chance to prove their capabilities. I remember when I started doing MLM, I was pregnant but still I was treated like all the other members. I was never made to feel out of place. Even after delivery I was able to take my son with him to attend presentations without any problem. The working hours are very flexible and most MLM companies have a large number of people who only do the business on a part time basis. This makes it easy for people to get involved because they are not forced to give up whatever they would be involved in prior. Therefore, people get to do their business after work hours or during their off days. This kind of business can also be done online 24 hours a day, which gives it an edge over the usual 8-hour shifts. It allows everyone to do the business during their most comfortable periods thereby maximizing productivity.

Portability

The portability part of the business is also another plus. Since word of mouth advertising is used, it means anytime and anywhere you meet people, the business continues. It does not require you to sit in the office all the time for you to work. Most MLM companies create a brief introduction of the company with the use of flyers and videos that make it easier to reach a wider crowd without necessarily wasting that much time doing the explanations. The advent of technology has improved this area many times than it was 15 years back. With the latest social apps, people are able to communicate in business group chats touching a huge number of people at once. The mobile phone also ensures that business is open almost around the clock. It simply means you get a chance to carry the business anywhere all the time.

Huge demand on products

It is an added advantage when the product or service that you are promoting is on high demand. With many companies, it is always the case. This makes the business much, much easier. Most of the time, it is products that are essential in our everyday lives; and we also become customers in our business, which is very interesting. As an example, when I was introduced to MLM I was in need of products for fibroid problems. So after getting satisfactory results from consuming the products I immediately became a staunch customer, purchasing repeat orders. When you are distributing a product not only for money but also because of its benefits; it becomes an enjoyable job. It becomes a life transforming career in different fronts. It is good to sell or offer a service that leaves people with great satisfaction. It definitely makes you unstoppable in business.

Unlimited returns and residual income

We are so used to trading our time for a salary that we often fail to see the potential of a residual income that MLM offers. Besides the money that you make from the once off sales, you also get a chance to benefit from the future transaction of all those that sign as part of your distributorship.

While in the corporate business, salaries of employees are pegged in correspondence with their positions and qualifications, MLM offers uncapped earnings that grow with your growth in business. The harder you work and the more productive you become means more money in your pocket. Basically MLM gives you a chance of deciding how much you want to earn as your earnings rise with your efforts. There is an advantage of residual income where you continue earning for your earlier efforts. In the corporate world it does not matter how hard you work; your pay will always be in accordance with the contract that you signed.

Attainable freedom

MLM gives you an opportunity to create a system that once smoothly runs; continues to generate income for you on a regular basis. It affords you such a fulfilling lifestyle normally enjoyed by the rich and celebrated ones. This is what most people dream of; so all the new members of an MLM company who have a clear understanding of what the company offers, will definitely have automatic motivation throughout their journey with them until they attain their financial and time freedom. After a year in MLM, I flew overseas several times, which is something that I had never imagined. I was able to easily earn up to more than ten times my restaurant salary of R3000 as a manager. I got my first car as an award from MLM. As of 2019 I managed to purchase a house at one of the up-markets suburbs of Pretoria after renting for so many years. My financial status was transformed in a very short space of time and for me MLM is the gateway to success.

CHAPTER 7

SERVANT LEADERSHIP

"Another important skill that you must master quickly as a servant leader is the ability to listen. Being a good listener enables people to have comfort in sharing with you their problems together with ideas that can benefit you"

One of the skills that will assist you in achieving whatever goals and success that you aim for in life is the skill of leadership. Unfortunately, it is a skill that is lacking so much in most people resulting in a lot of jeopardized projects, abandoned dreams and marvelous ideas being aborted before take-off. The immense pressures and responsibility that come with the post of leadership more often leads in many being found desperately wanting in that role. Looking at many different countries around the world, there are so many loopholes that can be pointed out and attributed to poverty that the masses still languish in. Leadership that has been poorly executed and deficient of the vital prerequisites degenerates into a disastrous crisis that destroys the lives of the following that is at its mercy. I have observed so many different types of leaders in action both as an employee and as a businessperson leading to my conclusion that servant leadership is the best.

LEADERSHIP IN THE FAMILY

Leadership must be understood that it begins with an individual. A person must be able to lead him or herself first before leading others. This means every individual must take responsibility; starting with their lives. You cannot expect to provide leadership to others when your life is in shambles. First fix yourself and show responsibility that will attract and draw other people towards you. Your behavior must be exemplary and modeled around good moral values that create an admirable image in society. The way you carry yourself as an individual says a lot about your character and capabilities. Do not be that kind of person who goes around creating trouble all over the place. Always be in a position to know what is expected of you as a person. Have good judgment skills that will help you to know what is wrong and what is right.

If you are able to lead yourself then you can provide valuable leadership to your family. Families and homes are the main grooming grounds for leaders and it is where your ability to provide direction becomes evident. As a mother or father you have a responsibility to produce and raise future leaders in your kids. A family whose structure is in shambles is bad not only for the children growing up there, but to the whole community. As a leader of your family, your duty is to make sure you provide the necessary support vital to the well-being of those who look up to you. When we talk about support, many people believe financial support to ensure the family is accommodated, fed and dressed is all that matters. However it must be noted that it goes further than that. The family needs psychological and moral guidance to help them become better citizens in life. As parents we need to understand that our kids rely on us for most of the things they need to know as they grow up and it is our duty to provide that information.

Nowadays career paths and employment separate family members for a long time creating a huge void in the area of nurturing and moulding our children. This results in children relying on colleagues and the media to get the valuable information that they need. It is because the absence of proper parenting leaves them with no choice. Busy schedules separate kids from their parents at a very young age depriving them of a great chance of acquiring knowledge, cultural and moral values. It is a gap that each parent has to make an effort to fill up and that calls upon your leadership qualities as a parent.

It is important again that we watch our behavior in the presence of our kids; because it is our actions that impart long-lasting impressions than our words. Parents who fight in front of kids must know that they are actually contributing directly to a culture of violence in society. Children who grow up in violent families become traumatized, filled with anger and hatred making them very likely to become violent also. That is what they learnt from their homes and they will go on to practice it too. How do we expect them to have an alternative way of handling issues and disputes when they were never provided with it in their early years?

The same applies to kids raised in families where parents always have negative thoughts and words. When you complain about everything in front of kids, you contribute to the creation of a society full of complainers. Do not expose your children to too much negativity. Rather than complaining, find solutions. Good quality leadership means being a problem solver and when kids learn that, they grow up to become creative individuals who think out of the box to come up with solutions. Nowadays there are so many cries about teenage pregnancy, drug abuse, and high rate of rape and murder cases including many other heinous crimes. We even have cases of kids killing each other on school campuses and many more who go to school armed with guns and knives. All these point back to poor parenting skills or total absence of parental guidance. It is failed leadership on our part as parents, a case of broken family structures contributing to a broken society.

It is rare to find parents sitting down with their children discussing careers and future plans. Most parents will only do so when something has gone wrong and they need to vent their anger on the issue. Our children must get ideas and advice from us as parents. How do we expect them to become successful business people when we have never given them advice about business matters? We never discuss with them legal and illegal ways of making money and then we cry when they learn these things from the streets and get caught up on the wrong side of the law. It is vital that parents reclaim their leadership positions in terms of parenting and providing guidance to children in order to produce better citizens.

LEADERSHIP IN THE COMMUNITY

To create better functioning communities, with less disgruntlement, improved service delivery in all sectors and a strong stance against criminal activities; we need to strengthen the leadership part. We must produce more leaders in our communities and the good part is we do not have to vote for them but groom them from a young age. The reason why we struggle so much with increasing problems is because we are not creating enough problem solvers. Be it at the workplace, at school, in church or any other section of the community, leadership or lack of it has a serious direct impact on the image of the particular institution. Most people get this issue of community leadership wrong by leaving all the duties to one person who occupies a certain position in the community while the rest neglect their duty. Every individual in the community has a part to play to ensure the desired kind of leadership is achieved.

I remember growing up in a community where as kids we were forced to toe the line, not only by our parents and teachers but also by any member of the community. You would not do any mischief in the presence of any elder and get away with it. It was highly impossible. The community members practiced hands-on parenting and leadership across the board and that helped to mould us to be better people. Nowadays the community has taken a back seat; kids do as they please while adults literally fold hands and watch. We have adopted a destructive line that says, 'as long it is not my child'. We need more people who will offer themselves as servants of the community with the sole aim of restoring normalcy in our land. A better society starts with you taking the initiative and doing your bit, we are all leaders in different ways and we must play our part.

LEADERSHIP IN BUSINESS

When I was introduced to the business world as a leader of my team in Multi-marketing business, I acquired a great deal of essential leadership skills that enhanced me as a person and upgraded my qualities. The moment I grasped the fact that my growth, development and success in the field were all centered how I led the team, I realized the necessity of servant leadership. I learnt that I had to act like a responsible mother to them who would make sure she feeds her kids first before she can eat. All servant leaders eat last because they understand that their strength comes from the teams that they lead and therefore they need to have them empowered.

Starting the business with a team of three members, I knew I had to master the process of duplication to ensure progress. This meant that all the information that I acquired had to be passed on to my partners on a regular basis to keep them on the same rate of development as me. This helped the team to grow in numbers in a short space of time. The duplication part is the area that crushes many who fail to adopt this tactic because of selfishness. Multi-level marketing is a game changer where you never succeed without making your team successful first. Your happiness in the business lies with the team that you lead. For you to get paid they have to earn and to achieve incentives, you have to help them achieve theirs first. It is a business where you grow by lifting others to your level. If you are a selfish leader who only focuses on personal achievements only, then you are bound to fail.

Once the team grew in numbers it was time to distribute and share leadership responsibilities by identifying potential qualities from members and entrusting them with the task of taking the work forward. This is a stage where belief and faith in others needs to come into play. When your team members feel embraced, they go an extra mile ensuring that they do not let you down. On the other hand if they feel there is a lack of trust from the leader; their spirits are dampened and performance is affected in a big way.

In all the markets that we established, I ensured that the same services were offered fully in the same way that I did at my centre. The presentation, training and motivational knowledge had to be effectively imparted to new members ensuring more recruits and sales. My main duty was to make sure I give all the necessary support needed in remote areas where the business had expanded to thereby ensuring continued sustainable growth.

As a leader it should be within you to see yourself producing people who live to surpass your standard and take the business or whatever brand that you are working under a notch higher. It is a critical skill that needs you to remove most unnecessary emotions and stick with the emotion of love. When you love your team members you will have no problem seeing the necessity of bringing them to your level and higher. You definitely want them to flourish. Most good teams are destroyed when leaders start to be in competition with their team members resulting in jealousy and hatred. Always ensure you avoid falling on this pitfall in your leadership style. Celebrate your team members' successes the way you would celebrate the success of your child because they are like your children. Make sure you recognize them for their efforts and achievements and if possible award them from time to time. This is the greatest fuel you can give to your team.

I still remember very well when I started awarding my team with small things like company branded t-shirts and caps; the results in terms of motivation and strengthening the spirit of unity. When we started organizing motivational events later they never hesitated to pitch up and do the same to their business partners. So it is always a great thing to spread the spirit of love as you grow in leadership. Never be too big or too special for the people that you lead; when you do that they obviously retaliate by detaching themselves from you in numbers and at the end of the day you are reduced to a lone walker rather than a leader. It is crucial to exercise professionalism and never take your team for granted. Yes I said treat them like your kids, but that was to emphasize the point on the kind of love you are supposed to give them; so never forget to show respect.

Your sterling leadership style is what will make you stand out above the rest of the rest and earn you enormous appreciation all over the places you go. When your good reputation precedes you, it becomes much easier to do business; be it making a sale or recruiting. Remember people are interested more in your image and reputation as a business person than the actual business that you are presenting to them. After they are convinced that they are dealing with the right person that is when they fall for what you are bringing. So in standing out you need to make sure you build a brand that sales you, your business and your team. Your brand must be appealing and envied by your team and prospects alike. All this relies on the quality of the leadership skills that you employ.

Another important skill that you must master quickly as a servant leader is the ability to listen. Being a good listener enables people to have comfort in sharing with you their problems together with ideas that can benefit you. Your position as a leader requires you to always come down to the level of following and hearing them out. When you have good listening skills you are able to take different views and suggestions from your team and digest them to come up with the best ideas for implementation. You also should be able to listen to the problems faced by the team and come up with lasting satisfying solutions; so it is important to ensure that you afford your team members the chance to talk while you sit down and listen. When you do this more often, you get a chance to acquire some valuable points while also assisting them with their grievances. Therefore, it becomes a perfect case of iron sharpening iron.

Above all make sure you stick to your mandate as a leader. Understand that you occupy the driving seat and your duty is to steer this ship through whatever rough winds and turbulence of the sea towards your destination. The team looks upon you to provide solutions for all the problems that arise. Therefore you need to be a problem solver of note. Do not despair or run out of ideas in the middle of the journey. Whatever you don't have you need to outsource from outside. Make sure you continuously provide vision and direction rather than weeping the loudest in your team.

Many leaders who get stuck along the way always point out a number of reasons for their failure. The most common one is always a blame directed to the people who were supposed to give direction. In my case I did not have anyone providing direction and instructions on a daily basis but I understood that crying over this would only result in me creating more crying and complaining amongst my partners. So I simply searched for whatever support that I was lacking from other people who were willing to provide. This ensured my team was well supplemented without even noticing that I was outsourcing these solutions as their leader.

Assuming leadership responsibilities must be coupled with the right attitude. Know that your failure has a bad impact on the entire team. Once you understand that, you are in the right state of mind to handle the magnitude of your duty. Your approach becomes that of a conqueror and no problem will ever be too big for you to solve. That kind of attitude boosts the confidence of your team. They always know and trust you to make a through way in dark times and before you know it this never says die spirit will live in your entire team. Never lose your footing as a leader; your eyes must always be on the target; the bigger prize. Know that there is no journey without obstacles, and your mantle as a leader is tested by your ability to create a way with your stride and leave indelible footprints that will give direction and guidance for many years to come.

CHAPTER 8

EXPECT AND EMBRACE FAILURE

"To some people a single unsuccessful attempt on something becomes the final nail in their coffin. They suffer from severe devastation and at the same time develop a phobia for failure".

Most highly successful people that you come across always have a story about their previous failure or failures to share. In most cases you will get to hear embarrassingly dismal failure stories on the same field where the person has achieved genius status. It becomes unbelievable for many people when they listen or read such stories and they are always left with questions as to how the particular individual ended up succeeding in a way that appears magical. It has to be understood though that all types of failures offer valuable lessons that can never be attained or accessed outside the experience of failure.

Whenever you hear the word failure or someone crying about having failed, there is one thing that you can be certain of that makes all the difference; that person has attempted. That should be a great motivation to the individual in question and observers alike. It is unfortunate that failure carries along so much disappointment that many of us never see the good part of this experience. Don't get me wrong , there is no sane person who sets failure as a target in their lives, but the fact of the matter is that there are millions of people who fail in one aspect of life everyday around the world.

I am one person who hates failure so much that whenever I fail on something, I suffer from insomnia, loss of appetite, weight loss, stress and many other things that you know. What I have learnt over the years though is that it does not help in any way to hang your head in shame and nurse your failure. Crying that you failed does not alter the results that you have neither does it assist your situation. The proven remedy for failure is to try again. Wise people refer to it as failing forward.

As long as you do not quit trying, you have not failed. A real failure is one who has thrown in the towel and given up on whatever dream they had. If you accept that failure happens to so many people all the time, it is easy to realize that it is a normal thing that can be encountered by all normal people. It must therefore be accepted as part of life. I would like to believe that it is actually part of the journey to success as I stated earlier most success stories are preceded by failure or a series of failures. Our reaction to failure that is more dangerous than the experience itself.

To some people a single unsuccessful attempt on something becomes the final nail in their coffin. They suffer from severe devastation and at the same time develop a phobia for failure. Once you are afraid to fail it simply means you have given up on trying which is a fatal mistake in one's life. Failure should provide you with lessons and experience to come back better equipped and stronger than before.

Even though I have stated that failure is part of the journey to success and part of our lives in general, I need to point out that there are always reasons for it. The fact that you did not succeed on something means there are areas that need to be addressed. In most cases, it is because you lacked something somehow or you were just not well prepared for the task. Sometimes we put on years of preparation and hard work but still go on to fail. It just shows that with all that preparation, there was still plenty room for improvements and upgrades. Wise people capitalize on that; they identify and correct wherever there are shortfalls and on so doing they are able to stage amazing comebacks that leave onlookers astonished.

Many people venturing into business or any other projects come across many obstacles on the onset; they often mistake those obstacles to failure, and end up aborting the mission too early. There are always challenges when starting any new venture and those must be properly read and not taken otherwise. In business, you first invest money, time and effort in its early days before it can flourish and start to give meaningful returns. You must be wise enough not to confuse a difficult phase of your business as failure.

In my case as a new person in business there were times when things appeared to be upside down and I seemed to be heading for disaster. Lack of understanding also made things worse. Then there was pressure from my partner who gave me all the reasons to abandon the journey. Some of the reasons he gave seemed genuine. For example he cited that since I was pregnant I was not supposed to take strain and stress of going around selling and recruiting. My family members also piled the pressure, telling me that this thing was not working. In one of those trying months I received payment of R37 and everyone around me had the same words, 'we told you'. I could have thrown in the towel any minute but what I understood was that I still had a lot to learn in order for things to work in the right way so quitting at that stage to me was the same as quitting before starting.

It is true that we experience some of our darkest hours just before success and if you treat them as the last straw you lose everything. For me the darkest moments awakened me to go seek the right information and it was not long before things started flowing and many of those who were encouraging me to quit were silenced. Sometimes you need to exercise the right amount of patience before you can consider quitting. Never hesitate to give it one more push all the time.

Many people start businesses and two or three years down the line they close down. That phase should be considered as the baby steps of your business and at that stage it is still far from being a failed project. Businesses grow stage by stage until they reach maturity. It is therefore important that you understand those stages and all the factors that come into play otherwise you will never have a successful business in your life.

This is simply to say to you that on your journey in pursuit of your dreams, visions and any other thing that you aim to achieve; you are going to encounter failure somewhere along the way. You have to be prepared to handle failure with maturity understanding that it is not the end of your journey. When I started a Multi-level marketing business, I gave my team the name of Must Achievers. We were giving ourselves ultimatums of achieving at all costs. We told ourselves that failure had no place in our team and achievement was a must. Along the way however, we encountered numerous failures and setbacks but we never allowed these to halt our progress. What we did not achieve at first attempt, we made our corrections and went for it again and that way we lived up to our name. We made sure we achieved at all costs. We managed to draw positives from our failures, taking those lessons and incorporating them into our journey thereby converting them to success stories. At the end of the day we achieved great things and most in our company believed that we were indeed must achievers.

In my private life, the story of my failed attempt on marriage also gives a good lesson not to give up. Like most girls I dreamt of living a happily married life and when I fell in love, it seemed like the dream had come true. When it became evident that my relationship was on the rocks, I desperately tried to make it work. I was so afraid to face the reality of being a failure to the extent that I had to suffer abuse in silence without telling anyone. I pretended that everything was going smoothly and I so much hoped that it would normalize. When it became apparent that I was fighting a losing battle, I was devastated but I chose to embrace the fact that it was beyond my power. I had tried all means possible to bring back sanity to the situation, including inviting elders to mediate and sort things between us but all that did not work. I had to accept failure and move on with my life. I did pick up the pieces tough as it was and directed my energy to more positive things in my life. I made peace with being a single mother of two boys and set out on ensuring that they get the best life possible. There are cases in your life where you will have to accept failure even though you are a success-oriented person.

All this having being said, I hope you are able to grasp the lessons that I am sharing with you. I am not encouraging you to fail. All I am trying to do is to equip you to handle failure in case you encounter it. In most cases our greatest fear about failure is how to face people who have been watching you running around chasing your dream. Do not be afraid to tell them that you have emerged stronger, wiser and more experienced. In whatever we do, let us not forget that success is a journey not a destination. Nelson Mandela summed it up when he said, "Do not judge me by my successes, judge me by how many times I fell down and got back up again".

CHAPTER 9

STOP HOLDING YOURSELF BACK

"For many wrong reasons and prolonged periods, we bear the heavy load of this useless emotional baggage in even sacrifice so much to make sure we take it along all the time. This in a big way slows down our progress and even affects our focus and concentration leading to our downfall".

From time to time in our lives we accumulate many unwanted items in our environment that take up a lot of space and need to be offloaded on a regular basis. That is why regularly our rubbish bins fill up and have to be emptied. It becomes a problem when something becomes useless in our life but we fail to realize that and decide to keep it anyway. It just sits there taking up space in the house or in the yard. When it is time to move to a different house we carry it along. We pay for it to be transported to the new residence, but for no particular purpose at all. We fail to realize that this particular item has served its purpose and we no longer need it in our life. I have realized that many times, quite a number of people experience this problem when it comes to their wardrobe. You will find a lot of clothing items that they no longer wear for different reasons but still remain in their drawers. Some of these items might have gone out of fashion long ago; others no longer fit, and some are even torn on a certain area. However they still occupy space in the house and when we do our laundry, they find their way into the washing machine, get ironed, folded and packed away to accumulate dust again without being used. It will take so much effort to convince the owner to throw such an item away or give it to those who will put it into use.

The same applies to our emotions. We accumulate so much emotional baggage in our lives and we create a bond with them; clinging to them as if they were a life support machine of some sort while in reality they are dragging us down. For many wrong reasons and prolonged periods, we bear the heavy load of this useless emotional baggage and even sacrifice so much to make sure we take it along all the time. This in a big way slows down our progress and even affects our focus and concentration leading to our downfall.

In your life journey, it is important that you work out ways of regularly freeing up your emotional space and avoid accumulation of useless costly stuff that will never contribute positively towards your progress. I have outlined a list of areas of our emotions that most are fond of clinging onto so as to help you out of that problem.

Fear

While it is normal to have fear when we encounter fierce situations; the most disturbing and crippling fear is the fear of the unknown. We normally create this fear in our brain when we are not very sure of what lies ahead. In most cases it is unjustified and normally based on our speculative thoughts on things that we do not understand clearly. After creating your vision and setting your goals, then comes the issue of fear to deal with. You start developing so many doubts about your dreams because you fear that they might never materialize. You fear that you are embarking on a project too big to handle. If you carry this fear for too long, it is likely that the whole vision will be deleted from your memory.

While fear affects every human being; it is the ability to handle it properly, focusing on recovering and getting on with your vision that matters most. You need to invite confidence by reminding yourself of some of the situations in your life where you emerged victorious in the face of fierce uncertainty. Carrying fear around all the time will make you rule yourself out of some of the critical life changing opportunities. It is a good thing to learn to overcome fear all the time and the best way to do that is to face your challenges head on. Whatever you fear needs to be faced and soon enough fear will fall.

Anger

Another baggage that many people like to carry in life is that one of anger. Some even brag about having so much anger as if it was a fashionable thing. People who carry around anger, lack peace. They don't only fail to make peace with other people but also themselves. Anger is the glue that sticks together all your disappointments and makes sure they are big enough to make you hold grudges and even seek revenge. Everyone gets angry at some point in life, but there is absolutely no reason to hold on to that anger and carry it around everywhere you go. Many times when you go around full of this anger, you end up venting it on people who never wronged you in any way. This is a bad thing for the people you interact with and also for your health.

There are people who hold on to anger for years or even decades. We have heard of cases of people seeking to settle scores about issues that happened during their schooling days decades later. How does this help really? I have heard of people vowing not to work or do businesses with certain individuals because of what happened long ago and they do stick to that promise. Meaning no matter how lucrative a business deal is; as long as it has to do with the begrudged person then they are out of it. If you look closely in such cases, the person who gets really hurt and becomes the big loser is the one holding on to anger and grudges.

At some point in my business life, I suffered a lot of setbacks and disappointments that made me an angry person. I was angry with the company, angry with my up line leaders and even angry with myself. I felt I was not provided with the necessary support and information to avoid some of the obstacles. Fortunately I got advice that opened my eyes to the fact that my anger was not going to take me anywhere. Whether I was angry or not the company was going to continue doing its business as usual. The lives of the people that I was angry with were also going to continue as if nothing had happened. So I was actually wasting my time and delaying myself in business by holding on to this useless anger.

If you want to make it in your business life and other avenues teach yourself not to have permanent enemies. You can be angry with someone today but find ways of making peace with them and getting on with life as there are always high chances that you will need each other in future. It is easier and healthier to get rid of anger than to live your life with a burden of entertaining it all the time. If everyone in the world were able to release their anger and grudges, the world would become a prosperous peaceful place to live in. We would not have conflicts, fights, wars and the only murders that will occur would be due to diseases, natural causes and accidents. That kind of a world would definitely be full of progress. It starts with you.

Guilt

We all feel guilty when we wrong others or when we go out of line and there is nothing wrong with that. There is also nothing wrong with admitting guilt as it opens the way for reconciliation and better relationships. However it is a problem to feel guilty forever and continue to take the blame for whatever mistakes you made. It is enough that you admit and the next step is to move on. Continued revisits back to the disturbing experience only kills your spirits and makes you appear like somebody who is incapable. Nobody is perfect in life and everyone has done something wrong sometime.

There are other instances though when we feel guilty without doing anything wrong. We feel guilty because of certain situations and people's perceptions or expectations pinned on us. I have had a lot of those experiences as a business person and working with a team. Sometimes you get to set targets that you want to work on together, with each person though directing their efforts on their own targets. At the end of the day not all of us will get the same results and those who did not manage to reach the target feel left out. They obviously feel used because they were also part of the group. This makes those who succeeded look like culprits; so this kind of guilt must not even bother you because there is absolutely nothing wrong with it. Remember when you succeed most people would be eager to find some faults in you.

So never let a sense of guilt stand on your way. Working as a manager sometimes it became difficult to execute my duties especially when I had to fire somebody. I would think about so many things; the person's family, kids and all the other expenses they would have to take care of without a job. I knew how it felt like to have no income but at the end of the day I had to follow the regulations and carry out the duties of a manager. So just imagine how many burdens of false guilt would I have carried around had I not been able to chuck them out of my conscience as soon as possible? Understand that it is no use going around feeling as if you owe everyone an apology for doing the right thing. So if you want to succeed do not hold on to guilt.

Blame

Another very common thing that holds us back is playing the blame game. Whenever things go wrong we have someone to point at or a certain situation to blame. While these things might be the real cause of your problem, it does not reverse anything to continue blaming them. It stops you from looking at solutions and different angles of approach that can make you progressive. Numerous times we find people complaining about their upbringing, the poverty they grew up in but all these things do not make them richer. It is just a waste of precious time and it becomes an easy comforting excuse for your failures. You need to learn to stop pointing fingers to other people for your own predicaments. People do not owe you anything and therefore your situation demands you to take action and find ways of getting around it.

In business we tend to blame the people we work with. We blame the staff, our clients, the government, the laws and many other things but not a single person has ever solved their problems by blaming. So laying blame on other people and making it your habit is a very useless thing to do. When you always have somebody to blame you miss a great opportunity to search yourself inwardly and do proper evaluation of your capabilities. Once you always think something or somebody is the problem, you will never find answers and solutions. So as you embark on pursuing success, get rid of the blame habit.

Ego

While it is good to have high self-esteem and be confident about yourself in whatever you do, excessive ego destroys the image of a person and makes them to self- important. The danger in this is that you start looking down or undermining other people which might as well be classified as disregard or disrespect of others.

If your ego is too high you might also end up missing out on some great opportunities thinking that you in a bigger league for them. I remember the responses that I always get from some people when I go around recruiting and selling my products. Some respond by saying their schedule is too busy for such things. While you get those who tell you that, they are not the type to go around selling products. All these people would be surely rushing to or from work and because they feel too special, they are not able to come down to a level where they can see business opportunity that can transform them from employees to bosses. Try by all means to stay humble and approachable even when you think you have achieved so much in life. Do not let the school that you attended, the clothes that you wear and any other thing that makes you feel special, stand on your way and cut you out from the rest of the people. Don't be tempted to throw around your weight or to handle your ego in a manner that becomes provocative to other people.

Loss

Spending time crying over everything that you have lost in life distracts your focus from the things that you stand a chance of gaining. We all suffer losses at one point in time. Sometimes we lose precious and endeared items, valuable assets, and even special people in our lives. Obviously such loses bring a lot of pain and misery. We look back and think, 'Had I not lost so and so, we would have done this and that together by now'. That stays as the reason why you did not go on to do whatever you intended to do. When you lose a person, either through relationship breakdown or through death, you need to accept that their chapter in your life is over. As long as you are not the only person left on earth, you can still find people to do things with. Of course you are not replacing the people that you lost; what you are actually doing is moving on with your life because it has to go on. No amount of tears about your loss will help you to recover anything. So get over it and focus on new things.

Financial problem

This one is more like a worldwide chorus and you will hear it in every street and corner. Off course employment is scarce but be innovative. It is a sad thing that our pursuits of a better financial life are hindered by the financial problems we face on a daily basis. It takes people with strong mentality to have the ability to rise above financial problems. Focus more on creating money-generating ideas that being stuck on the current situation. Many out there have abandoned their dreams and joined the wailing crew while the mentally strong have curved out their own ways and achieved wealthy lifestyles. Opportunities are in abundance out there, you just need to be alert and stop focusing on one area.

Many people find it unbelievable when I tell them that I started my Multi-level Marketing business with just R120. This opened my eyes in a big way and taught me to always be on the lookout for opportunities because they tend to show up in unexpected areas. The problem is that we have ways of making money, which have become traditional thereby reducing our chances of identifying those that fall in other categories. It is therefore an unacceptable excuse to spend the rest of your life crying about financial problems instead of working on finding solutions.

Jealousy

This ranks among the heaviest of items to carry around in your life. It needs to be constantly uprooted and thrown away as soon as it emerges. The useless part about jealousy is that it stops you from concentrating on your life as you spend too much time peering on other people's issues. Instead of being jealous about the success of others, the wise thing to do is approach them, seek advice and learn how they do it. In that way you will find yourself doing productive things. Most people who are jealous end up doing weird acts. First they will try to compete, later they try to sabotage the efforts of the competitor. When they cannot succeed in that then they try to stop the person. That is where we find some people going to extremes and killing others. The funny part though is that in all these acts of jealousy, no single one results in the transfer of whatever skills or achievement to the jealousy part.

Whenever you feel jealousy about anything, you need to immediately realize that you are developing evil feelings. Instead of useless resentment; it would be healthier and progressive for you to celebrate the successes of other people, learn and grow from them. It is unfortunate that it most cases people who become jealous towards us are those within our inner circle. We have seen even lovers, family members and friends developing evil thoughts towards the success of those close to them. If you aim to live a happy and successful life, make sure you cleanse yourself of any kind of jealousy, otherwise its weight will sink you and keep you down forever.

Excuses and self-Pity

There will always be plenty of things that block your progress. Do not dwell on them too much. Pick yourself up and move ahead. Stop feeling sorry for yourself because your life is 100 percent your responsibility. You have to stand up and overcome all the things that threaten to hinder your progress. There was a time in my life where almost all people that I came across easily read the misery written all over me. All the same I could not hang my head in shame. I had a business to run. Sometimes I had to travel to different provinces with my small baby. Most of the time, transport was a problem and I had to resort to hikes while carrying the baby on my back. I understood that the success of the business relied on me. Even though I had nothing to show, I had to gather the confidence to promise people free international trips, free car awards and many more. I had seen it happening and I trusted the company.

I had all the reasons to wait or postpone until a later time. May be wait for the baby to grow first or wait till I have my own car before travelling around, but I understood that those were excuses. The foundation that I lay at that time yielded great results at a later time making all the sacrifices worth it. I used to sometimes do three or more presentations a day not to mention scanning sessions. All that became my testimony later when I started achieving big things in the business. So I strongly advise people to stay away from excuses and stop feeling pity for themselves. It all points back at you. Would you choose a million excuses or a million dollars? Make your mark.

CHAPTER 10

STAND OUT, BE YOURSELF AND WIN

"Our success and winning spirit depends more in our mental readiness than the physical effort that we put. If we totally believe that we have the capabilities of conquering then we will act accordingly and channel all our efforts towards that goal".

Greatness follows a commendable track record of excellent performances, great strides against all odds and plausible efforts in different sections of life all aimed at taking you and the people around you to whole new levels. It is these sacrifices that help perch your profile high up there where everybody can see. The accolades that you receive as you complete your task diligently are a confirmation of the prolific winner in you. As an individual you need to always understand that you are unique and there is no other like you. You need to sometimes wake up in the morning and start by congratulating yourself for being a winner because you are already. Your winning streak started the day you were conceived in your mother's womb. The biological processes that occurred and the sequence of events leading to the crucial sprint of thousands of sperm racing towards the ovum affirmed your winning spirit.

The challenging journey saw most sperm die along the way. A lot others made it to the ovum only to find that it was no longer permeable as the deal had been sealed by you and the process of your creation began. So you out ran and out smarted thousands at that time when you did not even have limbs, muscles or a brain. Just imagine how much potential you have now as a mature human being. How many challenges you can conquer now that you have a brain, strong bones and muscles? How many deals you can strike and seal now that you have a mouth and ability to talk and communicate, negotiate and convince. So from the day you were born, you were already a champion waiting to be crowned.

Your duty is to stand out from the rest and make sure you claim your birthright.

So you were born with your work cut out for you. You were born with a mandate to fulfill. This is the reason why winning for you is not a choice but a birthright. Of course it has to be remembered that not all people live to claim their birthrights. It is those that will understand that it belongs to them and go on to protect and safe guard until such a time that it can be claimed. Those who fail to do so end up handing over their birth rights to more aspiring candidates unwittingly. A lot of those who lose their birthrights to others are often caught too pre-occupied with a certain distraction that they only realize later when it is taken. Others fail to read the times and situations. They fail to realize when to apply some sense of urgency on the matter. There are many other things that can stop you from claiming your winning badge and you need to overcome them one by one until you hold your prize in your hands.

When we look at the popular Bible story of how Esau lost his birthright to his brother Jacob, we always focus a lot on the deceptive manner in which the later won while ignoring some of the good aspects about him. We need to note that Jacob had a burning desire to inherit the throne. He treated it as if his life depended on it. On the day when the aging father was ready to pass on the throne, he made sure he was there. He made a plan to work with what was available at the moment for the mission to be completed. Those are some of the valuable lessons. You will not always have things perfectly ready for you to succeed. All you have to do is make a way, find a solution, sacrifice. So if you are hungry enough for it, you will make a way of getting it.

It is an obligation for every one of us to become winners like I have already stated. Now how much zeal and zest do you have inside you? How much determination is there in you and how big is that fire burning inside? These are the only things that will push you to your success and help you to cross the line and claim your prize. After travelling this far in this journey, you definitely have experience and knowledge on how certain things will keep you from achieving your dreams. So you are now more than ready to turn the world upside down for your birthright.

Be convinced first that you are a champion and a conqueror and that can be best achieved by pocketing all the small achievements along the way. When you have so much convinced then you have the confidence to wake up in the morning, look in the mirror and proclaim that the giant is up and raring to go. From there you need to dress up, step out of your comfort zone and face the other giants out there. We now know that words create, so whatever you say about yourself will come to pass. When you proclaim yourself as a giant, you talk like a giant, you walk like a giant and obviously act like a giant. There is no way that you are going to be intimidated by other giants out there.

Our success and winning spirit depends more in our mental readiness than the physical effort that we put. If we totally believe that we have the capabilities of conquering then we will act accordingly and channel all our efforts towards that goal. We do not have any slightest doubt about that. So you actually need to weed your thoughts, remove all the negativity that might arise.

Next you need to know that there is no winning without sacrifice. A lot of things have to be sacrificed as we have discussed in the previous chapters. They do you no good except hold you back. Now it is time to sprint towards the finishing line and there is even more to shed. It is time to shed those precious things that earlier on you felt like they are too important to leave behind in your journey. This you do by completely devoting yourself to the work at hand. Distractions no longer have a place at this stage and you just need to sprint like a blinkered horse.

As a new networker I used to envy fellow distributors as they went up and down the stage at rallies to collect their awards. I would always wish to be the next one. What I lacked was the full understanding of the route that leads to that electrifying moment on stage. Once I grasped that, I understood the sacrifices that come with it. The problem with many of us is that we like being on stage but hate the journey that takes us there then we wonder why we never get there.

In whatever you, do not forget that you are a winner destined for the best in life. There are situations that you will encounter along the way. Approach them with the mentality that you are the main actor in this movie. After all the strong winds and raging fires, you have to emerge from the debris and lift your trophy. The only thing that can stop you from winning is abandoning your journey. Forfeiting your birthright and that is just as bad as committing suicide. Never think of abandoning your race before claiming what is rightfully yours. Remember quitters never win anything and winners never quit. All champions have done something extra-ordinary in their lives. They encountered circumstances where they were told that there is no way out and they created their own way. Later their way became the only way, making sure their names stayed relevant for centuries. That is the mentality you have to adopt and employ on a daily basis.

This is the same mentality that has helped me gain freedom from the chains of poverty and given me undying will to succeed in all aspects of life. During my school going days all odds were against me as you now know my story, but it was the winning spirit that kept me going. I was always among the top five performing students in my class. I used to take seriously the comments from the teachers on my school reports. I liked and still like the fact that they gave an advice on which areas to put more effort and improve. They helped to identify the problem areas that needed attention in order to improve the results. They were never about doing better than other students but about doing better than what you have done before. That is what success is all about and it is the reason why I say winning should not always be about beating competitors but more about moving from mediocre to extra-ordinary.

In later years as an employee I managed to move from different levels in a short space of time due to the diligence that I applied in my work rate. I moved from the cleaning section to desert preparation and later to become a chef. It was no surprise when I was promoted to waiter then to work as a manager later in the same year.

When I joined Green World, it was a completely new world for me but it did not take long to relocate my winning groove and in no time, I was rolling again. After starting a distribution centre with a borrowed R5000, I managed to grow it to become one of the best under the company's Africa region headquarters in Johannesburg. This very shop went on to qualify for the 2015 Dubai trip award. Thereafter, I personally qualified for countless incentives of water purifiers and scanning machines. This was followed by more overseas trips to China three times, then USA in Las Vegas, Paris, Thailand and Australia. I also qualified for local trips around the African continent to places like Mauritius, the Portuguese Islands, and Pomene Islands amongst others. On top of all these, I managed to qualify for a total of seven car awards worth R87 700 each.

The success culture had set in with no doubt and as I scooped award after award in this fashion, it was a confirmation that I had built a very huge network of active distributorship. This is the team that together we have become a formidable force that never backs down to any pressure. My team is one of my treasured achievements and it is always a pleasure to see them going on to become strong leaders who do their businesses in an even more improved way. My goal of producing more leaders has been achieved with a magnitude that I never expected and it is always so fulfilling to observe the great work that the team continues to do. As I said before, I will always be around to make sure all their goals are realized.

With the backing of this team, I saw myself breaking some of the long-standing records in the company moving to the rank of 3 star manager within a period of four years. This is one of the revered ranks in the company and it comes with a whooping R1.5 million. My profile grew as a person with Nironence Moyo becoming a brand name. After being chosen as a star distributor for year 2017, I won the Miss Green World title in 2018. Then in 2019, I was approached by the company to become the face of cosmetic products advertising and up to today I still look at some of the posters with my face on them in disbelief. It just goes to show that there is nothing impossible in life if you have the right spirit and the right frame of mind. The growth of my name as a brand meant the growth of the entire team and Must Achievers today is one of the respected teams in Green world in many aspects.

As a fan of success, standing out and winning I found myself developing so much love for the South African national rugby team, the Springboks. My love is not so much of rugby as a sport but it has a lot to do specifically with the Springboks. When I look back in history, the teams' 1995 world cup victory cut across so many sectors of the South African communities, bringing unity and perfectly cementing the foundations of Madiba's rainbow nation dream. Their fighting spirit and conquering when most people viewed them as underdogs was an inspiring one. The entire nation of South Africa was left in a winning mood, going forward together in the same spirit. This team did it again in 2007 bringing the same positive implications to the country. The one win that will stay in my mind for a long time is the 2019 one, which led me to dig to their archives for more. I watched the game from the comfort of my home and I have no words to describe the amount of inspiration and joy that I got from that victory over a respected nation like England. The invaluable winning lessons displayed there from their fighting spirit and unity will definitely go a long way in transforming the way we do things as people. The amount of effort we need to apply and the pressure we have to absorb before we can lift our own trophies were all illustrated there on that pitch. This team also provides a clear example of how to become a winner and remain a winner with their consistence over the years.

The 2019 win came at a time when the country's ratings economically were not at their best and even though the win itself did not change the state of the economy, the motivation that came with it was a great remedy. For a moment people around the country took a break from their worries and indulged in much deserved celebrations that obviously became an inspiration and confidence booster. Other national teams in different sports like soccer, cricket, netball and athletics undoubtedly learnt a lot. They were left even more eager than before to also conquer the world stage in future. This win evidently cut across all fraternities up to the ordinary man on the street with the t-shirts and other Springbok regalia visible in every corner. People were brought together with a massive sense of belonging to a mighty nation. The hope and determination that came as a result of this is just invaluable.

All winners in life work extra hard and go an extra mile in whatever they do. They never lose focus of their goal regardless of how long it takes for them to achieve. When we win we inspire those around us. We inspire our communities and even our countries. So we owe it to all these people to stand out, step up and claim our potion of the spoils. Remember you are designed with all the necessary requirements for you to win.

Stop whining and win.

Stop procrastinating and win.

Stop measuring yourself against others and win.

Stop competing and win.

Stop waiting for the right time and win.

Stop limiting yourself and win.

Stay focused and win.

Run your race and win.

CHAPTER 11

FREQUENTLY ASKED QUESTIONS

This chapter deals entirely with addressing some of the most frequently asked questions about me, my business, my family including my private life. Besides all the other things that I have shared with you, these ones top the list every time people get a chance to ask me questions. They pop up during the questions sessions after presentations and trainings or in group chats. I also get them on general everyday talk. I felt they need special attention so that they can be addressed and help set the record straight on many issues. So the following are those questions and their answers in no particular order:

Question 1: Please share briefly your worst challenges and how you overcame all of them?

Response: My worst challenge business wise was failing to convince people to become my business partners. Then even those that did sign up lacked confidence in me so it was a struggle to develop under such conditions. The other main thing was lack of support from people around me. My family members were too busy minding their own businesses and my boyfriend who was closest to me at the moment was not willing to offer encouragement and support. So I overcame this by resorting to self motivation. I told myself that giving up was not an option. So every day I woke up and did some work while seeking information and that is when the team started responding.

Then in my personal life the number one challenge was that of losing my mother. It was so sudden and unexpected. She had not shown any signs of being unwell. So it was as devastating experience. I hoped that she would one day enjoy the fruits of my hard work. So that was very challenging. It left me heartbroken.

Question 2: Had you not taken the Green world business seriously, what would you be doing for living right now?

Response: I would most probably be working at a restaurant somewhere. Remember it was the only industry that I understood. I did not have any other qualifications or any certificates to enable me to go to other industries.

Question 3: How does it feel like to be a successful woman at your age?

Response: It is an awesome feeling and it makes me wish to share with all the ladies out there that starting early when you are still strong is the best thing to do. Work hard and hustle in your twenties when the energy is still high then you will have enough time to relax and enjoy later.

Question 4: How does it feel, seeing yourself achieving with others from your team considering your background?

Response: It is the best feeling ever to see the lives of these people being transformed in numbers. Some have flown overseas for the first time in their lives while others are now driving their own cars and have houses. I have a number of them who were so poor that they did not even have the R150 signing up fee. It is so satisfying, it gives me assurance that I am in the right direction. It is a humbling experience and let me state here that I crazily love them all and I will not rest until I see them achieving multi millionaire status.

Question 5: What were your strategies and what kept you going?

Response: I followed the basics in the business and acquired more essential information. So my strategies revolved around the two most important parts of the business which are recruitment and selling.

Question 6: How did you reach for the stars while parenting your two boys? And again when you joined Green World, it was not as popular as it is now, so how did you break through?

Response: Well for me the boys came as a motivation rather than a distraction. They gave me all the reasons to push myself harder every day and create a future for them. Then on the issue of breaking through, I relied on my testimonies to improve my confidence, firstly about the products, their later about the compensation plan. I made sure that my team members understood the importance of achieving. So we did everything on a massive scale. The cold market recruiting and outdoor presentations were all crazily massive. When I joined the company, it had been in existence for around eight years and I was so much eager to work hard and claim my portion.

Question 7: What motivated you to choose Green World out of the many companies offering the same services?

Response: I used the products and was cured of a sickness that had troubled me for years. I was cured from fibroids and cysts and managed to conceive. So the product efficiency motivated me to get involved. When later discovered I could also earn big monies through the compensation plan there was no stopping.

Question 8: what was your goal and did you achieve it?

Response: Well, I had set for myself a number of goals and I can safely say, yes I have achieved them. At first my main concern was being healed. Then later after getting fired from work I just wanted an income that would be enough for my expenses and supporting my mum. I earned more than that. Then my other dream of touring the world was fulfilled within 6 months in the form of free international trips. I was also my goal to buy a car and I achieved it. Then later it was a house and I achieved it too. Then the big dream of achieving along with my team, I achieved that also.

Question 9: What was your greatest fear when you started network marketing and how did you overcome it?

Response: There are many things that I was afraid of. Firstly I feared that I was not going to be able to recruit since I was shy to talk. So I was scared that I was not going to get new people fast enough to meet targets. I was scared that the business might turn out to be a scam I was very sceptical about it. So those were some of the fears. The only way to overcome was through gathering enough courage to face my fear. So I started going out to do invitation in the streets, I focused on gaining confidence as a presenter and went on massive campaigns and before long I saw the results. That is how I defeated my fear.

Question 10: In this journey to self-discovery what would you say was your greatest achievements so far?

Response: This journey has helped me to get to understand myself in an amazing way. It feels like I am a new person with revived energy and I am so inspired. I am so motivated that I can take on any task any day.